From Barber To A Business

The Simple Guide To Becoming A Successful Barber

Joshua Enoch

Dedication

This book is dedicated to a few people. The first person I am dedicating this book to is my wife, who has always supported me in every endeavor and helps me be the best me. Without her, there is no me.

The second person I am dedicating this book to is my mother, who had to play the role of a father and a mother, working three jobs to provide for me growing up. She is the one who gave me life by doing what she needed to do to make sure I was successful.

To David Williams, the first person who saw my potential in becoming a barber and pushed me to become better. He took me under his wings and showed me the ropes.

Unfortunately, he was not able to see my success and the seeds he deposited into me. He passed away a few years before I opened my barbershop. I believe God put him in my path to help steer me in the right direction.

Table of Contents

Introduction

Hello, I am Josh. I'm a 20-year experienced barber and the owner of Transitions Barbershop in Chicago Heights, Illinois. The reason for the writing of this book is a result of a high volume of barbers inquiring about the expedient growth of my business and the rapid building of my clientele. Let me explain. I had recently moved from Arkansas to Chicago in 2017 to start over. I was the owner of a barbershop, making six figures a year, and had created one of the first mobile barbershops in the world. I left all that behind to move to Chicago and I went from zero clients to cutting the heads of over 100 clients a week in under a year in a place I had never lived before. The barbers in the shop where I worked when I moved to

Chicago often asked me what I was doing. They were baffled at my success. After being bombarded with the same question over and over, I decided I should put the answers in a book, this book. The other reason I wrote this book is to educate students that are in barber college on how to be successful in this industry and provide tools on how to build as a barber. Many barbers experience the hardship of trying to make money when they graduate from school. This book will teach barbers how to manage their money, how to set goals and reach them, how to promote and brand themselves, and the importance of professionalism. I desire that this book helps you be successful as a barber.

Chapter One

My Story

I started cutting hair at the age of 14, out of my mom's bathroom in a low-income-three-bedroom apartment that she was renting. I began by cutting hair for only my close friends and people in my neighborhood, but by the time I was a senior in high school, I had developed a name for myself throughout the community. I was cutting hair for people I didn't even know. It was a way for me to make extra cash. Times were hard! My father wasn't around, so my mom had to work three jobs to provide for me.

Two months before I was to graduate from high school, a new guy moved in next door to my mom and I. He used to sit on his porch quietly and would never say anything to me. One day after finishing one of my friend's haircuts, I walked outside, and the guy kept staring at my friend's head. A tad bit disturbed at his awkward gaze, I asked him what he was doing. He asked me if I had just cut my friend's hair.

I answered, "Yes."

Then he said, "You can cut really good!"

He knew what he was talking about, he had been a barber his entire life and had even been an instructor at a Barber College. He asked me if I ever thought about going to barber college to get licensed. At that time,

I hadn't given much thought to what I was going to do in life, I was just trying to make some extra money, so I wouldn't have to eat free lunch. Free lunch was something they offered students that couldn't afford to pay for their lunch. School lunch was nasty until Friday, Friday was nacho day.

I asked him, "How much does it cost?"

 He responded, "It's only $3,100." He might as well have said it was $31,00 because I didn't have that type of money, and I couldn't conceive of any way to earn it.

The man I'm talking about was David Williams, he changed my life. He took me under his wing and showed me how to apply for scholarships and grants to get my schooling paid for. When I graduated from high school, I went straight to barber college. It took me a year and a half to finish. Upon graduating from Westark Barber College, David helped me secure a job at a good shop that paid well and allowed me to develop my skills. After three years of saving my money and at the ripe old age of 21, I opened my own barbershop. I was the youngest person in my city, and as far as I know, all of Arkansas to open a barbershop.

My Barbershop, J. Cuts, was open for 11 years. We were rated as one of the top 3 barbershops in the River Valley. We have also been featured in "Your Fort Smith," an online magazine. At J. Cuts, our mission was to create a relaxed and comfortable atmosphere for working-class men and students. We offered quality hair care services and we were known for our clean-cut style of cutting hair. We also helped the community by hosting annual block parties where we went to low-income based apartment complexes and offered free haircuts, food, bikes, gift cards, groceries, entertainment, and more. I grew up in a neighborhood much like the ones I am now able to give back to. In 2015, I launched one of the first mobile barbershop services in my state. It was designed to cater to the client and bring the barbershop experience to you. I have also developed the program, "How To Become A Successful Barber" which trains "up-and-coming" barbers and prepares them for the workplace.

Currently, I have 20 years of barbering experience and 17 years as a barbershop owner. I recently moved to Chicago and opened another shop. I changed the name to Transitions to reflect more of a brand than myself. I'm also the CEO of Barber To Biz, where we help educate, train, and mentor barbers to succeed in the industry.

NOTES

The Attributes of a Business-man

In this industry, we have a lot of barbers but not enough businessmen. A lot of barbers are skilled at cutting hair, but skills alone don't cut it. The characteristics of a businessman are a significant chapter to me because when you're coming into this industry, your mindset is the most important thing. In this chapter, I share with you the top four attributes a businessman needs to help him become successful in this industry. My goal in this chapter is to help you develop the characteristics of a businessman, but first, you need to see yourself as one. Whether you believe it or not, when you come into a barbershop as an independent contractor, you have become an entrepreneur. With this understanding, it's important you think like an entrepreneur and develop the tools you need to be better at being one. Being an entrepreneur is a mindset, we will unpack this a little more in this chapter. As an independent contractor, you must understand it's your responsibility to make sure you can pay booth rent and not the owner's job. When you can't maintain your booth rent, you are telling the barbershop owner you can't afford to occupy your space. Since you are an entrepreneur, you can't depend on the owner to get you clients, that's not his responsibility, it's your responsibility. It's the owner's job to run his business, not yours. The moment you became an independent contractor, you became an entrepreneur and now you must transition into a businessman. You are more than just a barber. You're a business and now it's time to see yourself as one.

Most barbers that fail in this industry fail because they don't have the right mindset. Their only goal is to make money. When money is your only goal, you will lack the other components you need to succeed. There are two types of mindsets you can have. You can have an entrepreneur mindset or an employee mindset, they're very different. In this segment of the chapter, I want to teach you the difference between these two mentalities. Let's begin with the employee mindset, this way of thinking focuses only on how much money can be made from behind the chair. The main objective here is on the work that needs to be completed and the efforts made from the hands-on work of cutting clients' hair. The employee mindset only understands the business as a place to work. They go to work, hoping they'll cut more heads and make more money. They rely on the walk-ins from the barbershop to make money.

The entrepreneur mindset, on the other hand, focuses on how they can grow their business and become better, they strategize on how they can keep clients coming back and keep new clients coming. The entrepreneur starts with a vision and plans on how they want their future to be in the business. They see beyond the money and the work that needs to be done. An entrepreneur understands that if they want to succeed, they have to solve their customer's problems.

Entrepreneurs listen to the problems of their customers and become the answer. That's one of the reasons why I got into the profession. I thought about the problem I had with my barber and how I had to run my barber down for a haircut. In my city that was normal for barbers and barbershops. They were never at work. This caused me to create a solution. I asked myself what would make me a successful barber. In this instance, all I had to do was come to work on time and leave on time. I didn't even have to cut hair. The fact that I was there, made me successful and gave me an edge over every other barber in my city. As a barber, you become by default, your client's non-degreed therapist. I would listen to my client's problems when they came to the shop. Customers liked the barbers in these shops, but they weren't professional, and they were never on time. Even the atmosphere felt uncomfortable. This created a desire in me to open my barbershop and become the answer to their problems. This is one reason why I usually encourage students not to open a barbershop right after they graduate from barber school. You need experience and some time to grow. No, I didn't like everything that went on in the shop I was working in, but I learned what to do and what not to do. I was learning what clients wanted their experience to be like when they came into a barbershop. The time of working in someone else's shop also helped to develop my character by submitting to someone else's vision. Do you see the difference? The barber only recognizes what he can do from behind the chair and the entrepreneur sees what he can do beyond the chair. An entrepreneur doesn't wait for the customer to come to him; they find creative ways to get the customers to them.

The first attribute that I want to talk about is vision. Vision is a dream or set of ideas and long-term goals. Vision defines the desired future you want. It tells you what you would like to achieve in your life. Vision is the ability to think about and plan for the future. Vision helps you see beyond what is current and launch you into the future you desire. Vision is what keeps you going when things don't seem like it's going the way you planned. Many barbers get into the industry and they don't know what they're trying to get accomplished. They have nothing that they are reaching for and they don't know what they want. Vision helps you see what you want and gives you an idea of what you need to do to get there.

You may be asking this question; "How do I write a vision" Well, I'm glad you asked! You first need to know what you want your life to look like in this industry in 5-10 years. In observing your desires over the next few years it's important to know your five- year plan, knowing your plan will help you understand where you want to go. Once you determine your purpose in this industry, then discover your reason for being in this industry. You may have to study the industry so you can know where you fit in it. So many people jump into careers they don't know anything about. They don't do any study on what they are getting themselves into. Lastly, you need to describe what success will look like for you and write down measurable goals. This may take you some time to decide, but it's necessary if you want to grow in this profession.

The second attribute that people in business need is a mission. A mission is knowing why you exist and understanding what role you play in a field. It's knowing your reason for being. It defines who you are, your goals, and what approach you're going to take to reach them. Ask yourself questions like, What am I trying to accomplish? Why do I want to cut hair? What do people need? How can I be different and what do I have to offer? There's not a wrong answer. You just need to know.

You have to define who you are and what you're going to be. When I got into barbering, my number one goal was to open a barbershop. I wanted to give my city a barbershop that would provide them with the experience that they were dying to have. I knew what I was aiming for. I knew my mission, my reason for being, and what was going to make me unique. My goal was to open a barbershop, my purpose was to give my city something they never had, and my uniqueness was to have a barbershop that was professional and gave customers a clean atmosphere where they would feel comfortable. Knowing who you are and why you exist gives you the drive you need to move forward.

The third attribute that a successful businessman needs is goal setting. Goals are statements of what needs to be done to implement a strategy. A businessman sets goals for what they want to achieve. If you don't have goals, you have nothing to aim for. You won't grow because you have nothing pulling you forward. You need to know what needs to be done to implement a strategy to reach your overall vision. Your goals should line up with your vision. You can refer to the following chapter on goal setting to help you with this.

The last attribute that a businessman has is a plan. A plan is a list of steps with details of timing and resources used to achieve an objective. It's an intended action through which one expects to achieve a goal. A businessman has a list of activities that needs to take place for them to achieve their goals. So, what is your game plan, your strategy, or master plan to get to where you want to be? If you fail to plan, then you plan to fail. You need an action plan. What are you going to do to get to where you want to be? It's not enough to have a plan. You must execute the plan to see any change. Goals without an action plan are dreams that will never be achieved. To sum this all up, a vision states what you inspire to become in the future. Your mission should reflect the past and present by stating why you exist and the role you will play in this industry. Goals are the more specific aims that you pursue to reach your vision and mission, and the plan is the strategy. Don't just get into this industry just to make money. Money is not the answer to success; progress is. If you make progress, the money will follow. People are not successful in life because they make a lot of money; they are successful because of what they were able to achieve. By adopting these attributes, you will be on your way to making progress and growing in this industry.

NOTES

28

Chapter Three

Goal Setting

Goal setting is essential. The reason why setting goals is important is because everybody wants to grow, but in order to grow, we must set goals and know how to reach them. If you don't have any goals, you can't grow because you don't have anything pulling you forward. One of the biggest keys to reaching your goals is writing them down, which is precisely what I'm going to teach you in this chapter. I have put together a strategic plan on how to set goals and reach them. At the end of this chapter, you will have a fill-in-the-blank worksheet that will help you with what I will be teaching throughout this chapter but let me start by giving you some statistics and percentages.

Science says, only 8 percent of people achieve their goals and 92 percent of people who set New Year's goals never actually achieve them. According to the study of highly successful people, you are 42 percent more likely to achieve your goals if you write them down. Writing your goals down not only forces you to get clear on what, exactly, it is that you want to accomplish, but doing so plays a part in motivating you to complete the tasks necessary for your success. The study also shows less than 3 percent of Americans have written goals, and less than 1 percent review and rewrite their goals daily. People who write down their goals are more likely to achieve them than those who do not. So, now that you know the importance of setting goals let's jump right into goal setting.

The first thing you need is a 5-year plan. What will your life look like five years from now? When writing down your 5-year plan, think about what you want to achieve. This will give you a clear perspective on where you want to go. You want to be able to determine where you are and where you want to be. The next thing you're going to do is write down some goals you want to accomplish based on where you see yourself in 5 years. Your goals should line up with your 5-year plan.

Then, you need an action plan for each goal you have written down. Years ago, I learned that if you fail to plan, then you plan to fail. Failing is not that hard, all you have to do is not do anything. I'm sure you have failed before, but reaching your goals requires hard work. It is critical not just to have goals but a plan for your goals. Nothing is just going to happen. The Bible tells us that faith without works is dead. What that means is that our faith is completed by our works. The truth is, you can believe whatever you want to believe, but if you don't have an action plan, it will never happen. Goals without an action plan are dreams that will never be accomplished.

Then you need sub-goals. Sub-goals are smaller goals to help you reach your overall vision or bigger goal. When working on your goals, don't try to do everything at once. Making progress is the most important thing. You don't have to rush to achieve your goals. The 8 percent of people who nail down their goals are smart enough to work on several smaller chunks to complete a big goal. They do this by knocking down one goal then moving on to the next one.

Once you have written down your sub-goals, write down one thing you can do each month to reach your goals. Then write down one thing you can do each week to reach your goals. Once you've done that, write down what you can do daily to reach your goals. This tip is the most important—those who are successful set daily achievable goals. You will find success by solidifying goals that are smart, measurable, attainable, realistic, and timely. Establishing small daily goals will help you achieve your vision more easily. To help you with this, write down one thing you need to do that you have been putting off for years, that one thing that can take you to the next level. Often, we know what we could do or should do that will help us get to the next level. We just don't do it.

Once you have that, you need to evaluate yourself monthly. You need to be able to track what progress you have made. Did you do what you said you were going to do daily and weekly? Do you hit your monthly goal? The next thing you need is accountability. You shouldn't be the only one who knows about your goals.

You should have friends, mentors, or somebody who can keep you accountable for what you said you were going to do. I know this is hard to do because we think that we don't need anyone, and we can do it all by ourselves. The truth is you need someone to push you and not let you slack off when times get hard.

Lastly, there are three things you should do with your goals daily. 1) Review them daily. Looking over your goals daily will keep your focus on them. It will remind you of what needs to be done to achieve them. 2) Meditate on them 15 minutes a day. You need to see yourself where you want to be. Meditation can bring you out of the fear of your goals not happening and bring you into the possibility of them coming to fruition. Meditation will also give you the endurance to keep pursuing them when you haven't seen your goals come to pass yet. 3) Speak them out loud. When you speak your goals out loud, you speak them into existence. Speaking your goals out loud will create an atmosphere for them to manifest. You need to confess what you want to see. Confessions are so important when you need to be motivated to continue with the action plans you have set in place. The Bible tells us that there is life and death in the power of our tongue. It's something about what you say that lines up with what you believe. Earlier in this chapter, we talked about your action plans and how faith without works is dead. What builds your faith to believe you can reach your goals is your confessions. If you walk around speaking that your goals are too hard and you're never going to reach your goals, then you won't because you have discouraged yourself with your confession and you won't have the faith for it. However, if you say things like, I will follow my plans. I will not fail because I plan to succeed; I will reach my goals because they are a part of me. You will strengthen your belief muscle and be much more motivated to pursue your goals. The Bible also tells us that out of the abundance of the heart, the mouth speaks. In other words, what we speak is what's in our hearts. You can tell what you believe about yourself and your goals by what you confess.

Understand that nothing is going to happen overnight. It may be painful now because you may not be where you want to be, but you can outlast your pain by moving forward. Your vision will live beyond the difficulty of your present circumstances. It won't always be this way, but you have to keep working on your action plans in order to come out of your circumstance. Make sure your goals have a deadline and that they are realistic. If you set deadlines and goals that are not realistic, you will only discourage yourself. Setting goals that are sensible and attainable will build your faith for the next level of goals you have because the truth is, you can't get to the next level until you have conquered the level that you are on. To sum all of this up, you need discipline. Discipline is the key to your success when it comes to reaching your goals.

GOAL SETTING

39

1. What is your 5-year plan?

2. What are 5 goals you want to accomplish this year?

ACTION PLAN

How are you going to reach these 5 goals?

1.____

____

____

2.____

____

____

3.____

____

____

4.____

____

____

5. _______________________________

____

____

SUB GOALS: (Smaller goals that will help you reach your 5 goals)

1. _______________________________

____

____

2. _______________________________

____

____

3. _______________________________

____

____

4.______________________________

____

____

5.______________________________

____

____

3. What is one thing you can do each month to reach these goals?

1.______________________________

____

____

2.______________________________

____

____

3.______________________________

____

____

4.______________________________

____

____

5.______________________________

____

____

4. What can you do weekly to reach your goals?

1.______________________________

____

____

2.____

____

____

3.____

____

____

4.____

____

____

5.____

____

____

5. What can you do daily to reach these goals?

1._______________________________________

____

____

2._______________________________________

____

____

3._______________________________________

____

____

4._______________________________________

____

____

5._______________________________________

____

____

6. What is that one thing that needs to get done that you have been putting off for years? (That one thing that can help you get to the next level)

Confession

I will follow my plans. I will not fail because I plan to succeed. I will look at my goals, speak them out loud and meditate on them daily. I will reach my goals because they are a part of me.

NOTES

Chapter Four

Professionalism In
The Work Place

In this chapter, I want to focus on professionalism. Professionalism is going to be a big part of your success as a barber. You cannot and will not expand beyond it. It's what keeps customers coming back and keeps your business growing. Professionalism is a combination of qualities and behaviors that demonstrate the commitment to effective performance. Being committed, confident, responsible, dependable, honest, and having a professional appearance. These are some excellent characteristics to have in this business. If you can be professional, you can also be unprofessional by not displaying the standard of behavior that's expected for your job. Professionalism will take you a long way. You must have some measures of expectation by working hard, being consistent, and having self-respect. What standards do you have? How will you conduct yourself? I have said this many times to barbers I mentor; "if you don't respect what you do, no one will." You need to manage your station like a business. Many barbers want their own shop but don't know how to manage the station they're renting. How can you own or manage a shop if you can't manage your station professionally? Here are some characteristics of professionalism in this business.

Personal hygiene. You want to be sure to maintain the cleanliness of your body and clothing. Dress well and smell good. When you dress well and smell good, it communicates to your clients that you're clean. You shouldn't be coming to the barbershop looking and smelling like the party you went to last night. Brush your teeth. There's nothing worse than getting a haircut by a stinky breath barber. I know this is common sense, but I've seen this happen on many occasions.

Be Sanitary. Keep your work area clean. Doing things like sweeping up around your station, dusting the hair out of your chair, using an antibacterial spray to disinfect your chair after every haircut, having hand sanitizer to use in between haircuts, and keeping your tools clean will communicate cleanliness to your clients and show them that you care about their wellbeing.

Respect your Clients. Speak to your clients when they come through the door. Greet them with a smile and use words like, "Sir" and "Ma'am" when communicating with them. Treat every client the same.

It's doesn't matter how long they have been coming to you. Give them the same respect you would give a new client. I have clients that I've been cutting for years that I still hand them the mirror to inspect the same haircut that I have given them many times. I even hand a mirror to my bald clients. Most of them will ask me why I always give them the mirror after all these years. It's because I respect them as clients. Your client should be more important than anything going on in the shop. You also need to make sure you are giving off the right energy. Clients can feel when things are off with you.

Have a good work ethic. Having a good work ethic can go a long way. Being on time, staying on schedule, having the right attitude, being reliable, being disciplined, and having integrity shows that you have a good work ethic. People with a good work ethic almost always maintain their professionalism. They exhibit a professional approach in the way they carry themselves.

Throughout my years of experience, I have identified four types of barbers in this industry. The first type of Barber is the lazy barber. This type of barber is the one who doesn't show up to work on time. He waits on clients to come to him. He's always turning down clients and is always late to his appointments. This barber usually blames the owner for not making money and is not able to pay his booth rent. Then there's the unprofessional barber, this is not always the case, but this is the barber who is skilled at cutting hair, but his time and professionalism are horrible. This type of barber seems to think because he is good at cutting hair that his clients need them so they will keep coming back to them. Then you have the unskilled barber. This type of Barber shows up on time and does everything professionally, but they have not perfected their craft. This barber tends to be humble and is doing everything they can do to perfect their work and get better. Then you have the professional barber. This barber has perfected his craft and professionalism. They go the extra mile to please their clients. They are developing themselves and are more likely to become a shop owner.

Now I'd like to pause here and leave you with this question, 'Which one are you and which one will you become?"

NOTES

Getting Down To Business

How you operate your business is going to be the key to your professionalism. Business has a system, and that system works if you work it. Whether you are doing appointments or walk-ins, you need to have a way that you do business. What will be the hours of operation for your business? What days of the week are you going to be open and closed? Remember, you're not just a barber; you're a business. There are two ways that barbers operate, by appointments and by walk-ins.

Let's take a look at how they work and what professionalism would look like in each function.

In my business model and my professional advice, appointments are the most professional way to do business. Your clients won't have to wait, they can come at their appointed time and you don't have to overwork yourself. If you're going to work by appointment, you need to have set hours. Your clients need to know your hours of operation. It's important to stay on schedule while giving your clients a grace period. However, if they miss the grace period, offer to give them an option to reschedule. If you stick to your schedule, your clients will respect it. If not, they will not. There's no point in your clients booking an appointment, and they still have to wait for hours to get a haircut because their time was pushed back due to their tardiness. Provide a cancellation fee. Cancellation fees will place a desire in your clients to respect your time. In keeping with a schedule, you also want to allot a specific time frame for your breaks. You don't want to have clients waiting on you while you're eating during their time slot. To maintain professionalism, create a way to communicate with your clients. Booking apps like Booksy, Styleseat, and The Cut can help you manage your business. They handle your schedule, log your clients, send out texts and email reminders to your clients for you. These apps can also take payments, keep track of your income, and they even have options for you to promote yourself. If you're a new barber, walk-ins are good if you are in a high traffic barbershop. If you're not in a high traffic area, you might struggle to pay booth rent. A lot of money can be made by accepting walk-ins, but you would have to grind and work harder to see the type of money you desire.

When I first started cutting hair, it was a great experience and the money was good. My challenge in this new place was, as I grew as a barber it was too much to handle. Many times, I would end up working longer than expected. The pros to receiving walk-in clients are good, but the cons to it are that you can overwork yourself. One of the things I love about appointments is that you can have a time slot and charge more money while cutting fewer heads. While the walk-in clientele is great, you should endeavor to have set hours of operation. If your business hours are 9am to 6pm make sure you are there. Your clients shouldn't have to guess if you are going to be at work or not. People need to build trust with you, and this is an excellent way of building your clientele. If you want to generate more money, consistency is necessary. Avoid leaving early just because you made a certain amount of money.

Develop a system so that when you are busy your walk-in clients can still be prioritized, and you can always know who is next to your chair. You may even need a sign-in sheet, so clients can sign their name in as they arrive. Perhaps this sounds like a lot, but this is what it takes to operate professionally and have longevity in this business.

I'm often asked which option is best when paying for your rental space at a barbershop, booth rent, or commissions. Booth rent is paying booth rental for the month or each week and commission is where a percentage of what you make goes to the shop. My answer, "Both are good." I offer both in my shops. I advise you to make your decision based on what you, as a barber are aiming for in your business. You must evaluate where you are and where you are desiring for your business to go. If you're fresh out of school, you may want to consider offering commission so that you don't have the stress of trying to pay booth rent at the end of each week. Commission gives you time to grow and allows you to take money home; with booth rent, you may not, if you're not cutting enough heads.

I recently had a discussion with a barber who had just graduated from barber college and was struggling to pay booth rent. He asked me should he pay his booth rent or should he use it to pay his bills? My answer was, "Pay your booth rent."

Shocked he asked me, "Why do you say that?"

It was a teachable moment as I explained to him, "If you don't pay your booth rent, you won't have a place to work to pay your bills." I further explained that he may need to consider being on commission. If he were on commission, then he would be taking home a percentage of what he made to pay his bills. See, when you're an independent contractor, you have to promote yourself. You can't just sit and wait for walk-ins to come through the door. If you know the direction you desire to go then you will make the right decision on whether you should choose commission or booth rent.

NOTES

63

Chapter Six

Social Media Marketing

In this chapter, we will navigate through my journey of moving from Arkansas to Chicago and how I went from having no clients to cutting the heads of over 100 clients a week in a city I never lived in by using social media. In this discussion, you will learn how to market, promote, and brand yourself using social media marketing. You can be the best barber in the world, but if no one knows it, you will lose out on clients and money. We live in a world where everything is digital. People are on their phones every day all day. You have to find a way to be in their face when they open their phones. Twenty years ago, when I started barbering, we didn't have these social media platforms we have now. Social media has made it quite easy to get our products out there and a way to connect with people we don't know. People will get to know you by what you post on social media. The type of clientele you want should be reflected in what you post. You will attract what you post.

There are a few things you need to understand when running ads on social media to see a return on your paid marketing. You don't want to pay for ads and not see a return. I see barbers all the time running ads that don't make any sense. They're only running ads to get more followers, but more followers doesn't always mean more clients or money. There are a lot of barbers that look good on social media and have a lot of followers but are not financially successful. I know millionaires that have less than 500 followers on social media. Don't be fooled by what you see; the only thing that matters is your return. I'm going to show you how I became a 6-figure earning barber by using Instagram.

The first thing that's important to know when it comes to branding yourself; you have to make sure your brand lines up with what you are promoting. You should only be posting content that aligns with your brand. When you explore my Instagram pages you will discover that I post pictures of clients whose hair I've cut and nothing else. I only share the things on my Instagram that expose what I do or what I want to encourage people to do. What you post matters, it's how people will view you and determine what type of clientele is attracted to your page and your business. When you are self-employed, you are your business, and how people perceive you matters.

There are plenty of apps out there that can help you create a nice image like Canva, Face App, and many more. Don't look cheap. Use bold and vivid colors that catch the eye, like yellow, blue, and red. Post your best work. You want to make sure the haircuts you're posting are eye-popping. Even if you don't think your haircutting skills are where you'd like them to be, I encourage you to post pictures anyway.

Your clientele will grow as you grow. Your clients will grow with you. Avoid posting other people's work. It's nothing like a barber posting someone else's work just to get clientele. The potential client needs to know exactly what they're getting when they come. Make sure your content is clear and straight to the point, they need to know what you want them to do as soon as they see your ad. If they have to pause their engagement too long, you're going to lose them. You only have a few seconds to grab the attention of potential clients. The busyness on social media has conditioned people not to read. Make it easy for potential clients to book appointments on your social media platforms. If it's too complicated, you will lose them. They should be able to click one button that takes them to your booking site or your information. Instagram has a book now action button that you can add to your ads that potential clients can click on to access your booking site.

Know your target audience. You need to know who you are marketing to. What is their age group, race, and demographic? You need to know who you are trying to reach. You can't reach everybody, but there are clients for you. Social media is oversaturated with talented barbers and it can seem overwhelming at times. That's why it's essential to know your target audience. If you try to reach everybody, you will waste money on ads and lose out on clients. I can't tell you how many times I've seen barbers running ads in states and cities that they don't live in just to get followers. It makes no sense, and they are wasting their money. If you are going to run ads, you need to do it within a 5-mile radius from where you work. A 5-mile radius will increase the number of potential clients that will see your ads.

You're more likely to grow your clientele a lot faster because the ads will run closer to where you work. Be as specific as possible. The more detailed you are and zone in on your ideal market, the higher your chances of reaching potential clients.

Use hashtags. People use hashtags to search for what they're looking for. Hashtag every post you make. You should hashtag anything you think people would hashtag if they were looking for a barber. Hashtag the city, state, and shop your cutting in. You also want to use hashtags that have a lot of tags because more people will see your post.

NOTES

Chapter Seven

Money Management

Let me start by telling you that 85-90% of barbers retire broke. That is a high percentage for a billion-dollar industry. What that means is that most barbers are living for the moment and not the future. If you live with the future in mind, you will be mindful of your money and where you're spending it. We live in a time where people want instant success and gratification. No one wants to go through the process. Growing your money is a process. No one wakes up and instantly becomes a millionaire unless they hit the lottery. But what are your chances of that? Wealth is built over time. There's no quick way to being wealthy or becoming a 6-figure earning barber. It's doing the right things constantly and making adjustments when needed that will cause you to be successful in anything that you're doing. If you want to be able to benefit and have something to show from the hard work you have been putting in, you have to have a plan for your money. If you don't have a plan for your money, something or someone will, but you have the power to tell your money what to do. We will talk a little more about that later in this chapter. It's going to take some discipline to get to where you want to be financially. You must understand that this will not just work because you read it. You have to put in the work and allow time for your money to grow. Again, there is no quick way to succeed. You will not become a 6-figure earning barber overnight; most people that are successful will tell you that they worked hard for years before they saw any success. I used to wonder how actors, comedians, bloggers, and other artistic professionals blew up or came out of nowhere only to find out that they have been grinding for years and finely got their big break.

In the remainder of this chapter, I want to layout principles I have been applying to my life for years and have seen the benefit of it. I don't believe in teaching people how to do things that you haven't done yourself. These are concepts I have been utilizing and I still apply to my life today. They're proven and will work for you if you employ them in your life as well.

1. The best way to manage your money is to determine your income. You need to know what you're bringing in monthly, weekly, or daily. You need some way to track what you are making. There's a couple of ways you can track your income, but you first need to know that every day is not payday. It is easier to determine what you're making if you are not spending money throughout the day. Set up a

payday for yourself, whether that be weekly, bi-weekly, or monthly. I prefer weekly. Have somewhere to put your money, so you don't spend it. Opening a checking account is an excellent way to determine your income. When you open a checking account, deposit everything that you make daily and then get statements from your bank showing what you made for the month. Another way is by writing down the money that you receive for each haircut; if you keep the cash on you, you're most likely going to spend it.

I had a barber in my shop who was struggling to pay his booth rent. He was cutting about five heads a day, and he couldn't understand why he was not making enough money. One day, we decided I would keep the money for him and pay him at the end of each week. This plan worked. At the end of each week, John was making between $500- $600 a week. During this time,

John was disciplined and didn't let his friends and family borrow money, he also wasn't spending money on whatever he wanted to until the end of the week. Do you see the principle in that? John couldn't spend money until the end of the week. It not only helped John track what he was making, but it also helped him track where he was spending his money, which brings me to my next point.

2. Tracking your money is vital when trying to build your money for the future. You have to know where your money is going and be able to ad-

just when needed. Just like John, most of his money was being spent on his friends and family borrowing money. He was able to adjust once he realized that's where his money was going. One of the ways you can track your spending is by using a debit card every time you spend money. Using the same method, you used to determine your income, but now you're

tracking it. This method will only help if you are depositing every-thing, you're making into your checking account. By doing this you will be able to track what you are spending your money on. Remember that you need to track everything that you are spending so that you will have accurate numbers. It's going to take some discipline if you want to build your money for the future. Once you have determined your income and tracked your spending, you need to set budgets based on what you have to spend.

3. Setting budgets for your necessities will help you determine where you want your money to go. At the beginning of this chapter, I talked about how you have to have a plan for your money. It has to have something to do to grow. If you don't have a plan for your money, some-

thing or somebody will. Think about it; commercials

and ads are running all day on TV and social media trying to get you to buy something, this is because they have a plan for your money. However, you have the power to tell your money where you want it to go.

One of the methods I use to set budgets is managing my money daily. I used to manage my money weekly by putting everything I made for the day into an account and paying myself weekly. That was an excellent method, but with that method, I still ended up spending more money than I expected. It was hard not to spend money throughout the week when you have money that you made for the day just sitting in one account because things come up. So, I decided to manage my money daily instead. Sometimes we can get into this illusion that we have more than what we have. By managing your cash daily, you can take account of the money that you spend that you're not even mindful of. It's easy to spend money on vending machine items in the shop, letting people borrow money, and buying lunch every day. You may think budgeting is being cheap, but I call it being smart. One of the ways you can manage your money daily is by having multiple banking accounts that you can transfer money to the specific needs or budgets that you may have. You can create a budget for shopping, eating, groceries, family, bills, and booth rent. By doing this, you can keep an account of where your money is going.

Remember, your money must have a purpose. It must have something to do, or it will leave easy, and you won't know where it went. Your money can be building your future, or it can be instant gratification. Mobile banking apps have made money tracking very easy to do. Let's say you make $300 a day working five days a week, that is $1500 a week, and your monthly bills and expenses are $4000 a month. You can break the expenditures down to daily percentages based on what your outflows are, transferring your daily percentages to each one of your expense accounts from the $300 that you made so that by the end of the week or month, your expenses would have already been paid. Managing your money daily will also help you to know what you have left-over to spend.

4. Once you have set your budgets, find ways to save some money. This is money you don't touch. The goal for saving is to save a small portion of your money that will grow over time. So, by the time you retire, you will have something to show for your hard work. The goal is to have saved up enough money to cover 6-12 months of your bills so if something happens where you unable to work, you will be okay. This allows you to create breathing room financially if you need to take a break. You don't want to be living cut to cut. I have created a five-year savings chart that will help you

build your money using a 10% calcu-
lation based on what you will make
daily. Let's say you work five days a
week and cut five heads a day at
$20. That would equal up to $100
daily: you would save $10 (10% of
the $100) a day, that would equal up
to $50 a week, $200.00 a month,
$2,400.00 a year, and $12,000.00 in
five years. You would save 12,000 in
5 years by just saving $10 a day.

I'll be honest with you, as simple as this is,
it's harder than you think if you don't have
discipline. I know you've heard the saying
it's better said than done.

At the end of this chapter is a five-year saving chart that I've created that you can fol-

low that can help you build your money. I also created a form that you can customize your savings based on what you are currently making. Saving money isn't just a principle I took out of a book and am giving it to you but a law that I have been applying to my life for years and have seen the benefits from it. If you follow this plan, you will be on your way to building your money.

A BONUS OFFER: Since we're talking about money, I wanted to add this as a bonus. I speak to barbers all the time about the struggle of paying their booth rent. I think your booth rent should be the first thing you pay. I believe it's more important than your bills at home. Because paying booth rent provides a place for you to work to be able to pay your bills. I think you should have a daily budget for your booth rent, just like you have a budget for your bills. If your booth rent is $150 a week, set aside $25 a day if you can. Don't wait until the end of the week when rent is due to come up with the money to pay it. Most barbers will work all week and then rely on one day of work to pay their booth rent. You should stay ahead of the game. When I was an independent contractor; I would strive to pay my rent monthly so that I wouldn't have to pay it weekly. But that meant that I had to be more disciplined with my money.

If I could summarize this chapter for you, it would be one word, discipline. You can have all the information you want, but it takes discipline to execute it. Hopefully, this book has helped you as a barber or someone wanting to be in this profession. My goal was to give you my 20-year experience in this book.

5 Year Savings Plan

$ Per Cut	# Cuts Per Day	$ Saved per Day	$ Saved Per Week	$ Saved Per Month	$ Saved Per Year	$ Saved in 5 years
$10.00	5	$5.00	$25.00	$100.00	$1,200.00	$6,000.00
$10.00	6	$6.00	$30.00	$120.00	$1,440.00	$7,200.00
$10.00	7	$7.00	$35.00	$140.00	$1,680.00	$8,400.00
$10.00	8	$8.00	$40.00	$160.00	$1,920.00	$9,600.00
$10.00	9	$9.00	$45.00	$180.00	$2,160.00	$10,800.00
$10.00	10	$10.00	$50.00	$200.00	$2,400.00	$12,000.00
$10.00	11	$11.00	$55.00	$220.00	$2,640.00	$13,200.00
$10.00	12	$12.00	$60.00	$240.00	$2,880.00	$14,400.00
$10.00	13	$13.00	$65.00	$260.00	$3,120.00	$15,600.00
$10.00	14	$14.00	$70.00	$280.00	$3,360.00	$16,800.00
$10.00	15	$15.00	$75.00	$300.00	$3,600.00	$18,000.00
$15.00	5	$7.50	$37.50	$150.00	$1,800.00	$9,000.00
$15.00	6	$9.00	$45.00	$180.00	$2,160.00	$10,800.00
$15.00	7	$10.50	$52.50	$210.00	$2,520.00	$12,600.00
$15.00	8	$12.00	$60.00	$240.00	$2,880.00	$14,400.00
$15.00	9	$13.50	$67.50	$270.00	$3,240.00	$16,200.00
$15.00	10	$15.00	$75.00	$300.00	$3,600.00	$18,000.00
$15.00	11	$16.50	$82.50	$330.00	$3,960.00	$19,800.00
$15.00	12	$18.00	$90.00	$360.00	$4,320.00	$21,600.00
$15.00	13	$19.50	$97.50	$390.00	$4,680.00	$23,400.00
$15.00	14	$21.00	$105.00	$420.00	$5,040.00	$25,200.00
$15.00	15	$22.50	$112.50	$450.00	$5,400.00	$27,000.00
$20.00	5	$10.00	$50.00	$200.00	$2,400.00	$12,000.00
$20.00	6	$12.00	$60.00	$240.00	$2,880.00	$14,400.00
$20.00	7	$14.00	$70.00	$280.00	$3,360.00	$16,800.00
$20.00	8	$16.00	$80.00	$320.00	$3,840.00	$19,200.00
$20.00	9	$18.00	$90.00	$360.00	$4,320.00	$21,600.00
$20.00	10	$20.00	$100.00	$400.00	$4,800.00	$24,000.00
$20.00	11	$22.00	$110.00	$440.00	$5,280.00	$26,400.00
$20.00	12	$24.00	$120.00	$480.00	$5,760.00	$28,800.00
$20.00	13	$26.00	$130.00	$520.00	$6,240.00	$31,200.00
$20.00	14	$28.00	$140.00	$560.00	$6,720.00	$33,600.00
$20.00	15	$30.00	$150.00	$600.00	$7,200.00	$36,000.00

Calculations are based on saving 10% of each hair cut and working 5 days per week

5 YEAR SAVINGS PLAN

Estimated Price per Haircut: $ _______________

Number of Haircuts per Day: _______________

Amount made per day: $ _______________
(multiply $ per cut by # of heads per day)

Amount made per week: $ _______________
(multiple amount of money made per day by number of working days per week)

What percentage of your earnings do you wish to save daily? (10%, 15%, etc…) _______________

Amount of money saved daily (convert to decimal):   10%= 0.10   15%= 0.15   20%= 0.20

$ _______________   X   _______________   =   _______________
$ Eearned each day   Percentage to save $ Saved Daily
                         (Convert to decimal)

Amount of money saved weekly:

$ _______________   X   _______________   =   _______________
$ Saved daily (from above)   # Days worked per week $ Saved Weekly

Amount of money saved monthly:

$ _______________   X   **4**   =   _______________
$ Saved weekly (from   (4 weeks in a month) $ Saved Monthly
above)

Amount of money saved yearly:

$ _______________   X   **12**   =   _______________
$ Saved monthly (from   (12 months in a year) $ Saved Yearly
above)

5 YEARS SAVINGS:

$ _______________   X   **5**   =   _______________
$ Saved yearly (from   (5 YEARS) $ SAVED IN 5 YEARS
above)

NOTES

NOTES